PIONEERS

A Guide to Parenting
in the Age of Social Media
and Gaming Addiction

Written by Seth Taylor

ISBN: 9781791948559

"*Through the blur, I wondered if I was alone or if other parents felt the same way I did - that everything involving our children was painful in some way. The emotions, whether they were joy, sorrow, love or pride, were so deep and sharp that in the end they left you raw, exposed and yes, in pain. The human heart was not designed to beat outside the human body and yet, each child represented just that – a parent's heart bared, beating forever outside its chest.*"

Debra Ginsberg

Introduction
Uncharted Territory

As my kids have grown up over the years, I notice how much I say things that my parents said to me. I even caught myself using the classic line, "When I was growing up, we didn't have (fill in the blank)." In those moments, I have to laugh at myself – not at my programming from my childhood or some funny memory. I finally noticed that a lot of parenting philosophies try to bridge gaps between parents' understanding of their own world and upbringing, and that of their kids' world. I didn't grow up in a digital world shaped in real time and designed to fill every gap in my consciousness. Sure, when I was a kid, very smart marketing people sat in a board room somewhere, strategizing on how to get their product into my susceptible little mind and heart in any and every way possible. But they had limited channels available to them: radio, television, movies, and print/paper (my god, paper!). The internet existed, but it was limited in its scope.

These days, the avenues to kids' hearts and minds are unlimited. Perceived necessity makes people darn-near-cybernetic beings, tethered 24/7 to a digital world. Adults experience this as the new normal, but kids' vulnerable minds and hearts – their egos and spirits – have to mature and form in this environment. The world creates and sells an unconscious, fundamental illusion: constant happiness is yours for the taking if you can fit the mold. And the mold is created on social media and in the hyper masculine world of video games in real time every day.

Before you get too depressed, take heart. This is not a doomsday book that tries to scare people into moving their families to a remote island in Alaska to live in a yurt, while teaching their children survival skills and classic Latin. Actually, this guidebook does quite the opposite: it empowers people to create a spectacular future with their kids, full of hope and possibility. This interactive guidebook provides the means, method, and awareness necessary to balance the excessive narratives that blast kids, looking primarily at video games and social media: the two arenas that have the most appeal and the most potential for addiction in kids. Yes, billions of dollars and armies of very smart people drive these industries, but I hope you discover an amazing fact through this process: no amount of money or army of techies can hold a candle to the influence a parent's love has over their child. It's not even close.

Buried in this maze of technological smog lies a key to your child's heart. This guidebook experience will help you find and apply that key in a way that empowers your child.

How to Use This Guidebook

This Guidebook is a collection of teaching, guided journaling, and action-driven exercises. These exercises will help raise your awareness of what happens in your unconscious – the deep parts of you that always try to get their needs met, but that you might not consciously know about. The higher your awareness regarding why you feel the way you do about your child's experience, the more clearly you can see the way forward. The great Psychologist Carl Jung said that 70% of what people do every day comes from the unconscious. Bringing that unconscious world into the conscious world through your attention and awareness helps you become the most intentional and influential presence possible in the life of your child.

You will be guided through three sections designed to progress you towards that goal. The steps will focus on how you and your child feel, think, and act in relationship to social media and gaming. Just follow the simple instructions and do your best to take a mindful approach to this experience for maximum benefit. Take your time and don't make getting to the end some sort of objective. The process resembles guiding your kids: it is a canvas to paint, not a dragon to slay. And your kids will be ok, I promise. How do I know that? I know that because you are reading this. You are awake and courageous enough as a parent to step up and take action about the world in which your child lives. And, as an intentional and awake parent, you are a powerful instrument for culture change.

Defining Terms

This guidebook employs a number of terms often associated with psychology and other academic disciplines, but since those terms tend to function differently in different contexts, we must define certain words for our purposes here.

Ego:

Ego is a psycho-babble word that gets tossed around in various psychology, philosophy, and spiritual circles. If you ever took Psych 101, you likely heard about Sigmund Freud and his famous examination of this part of the psyche. For our purposes, we use and define the word ego as the part of the psyche in charge of your survival: the reptilian brain, primitive caveman-like part of you. The ego has only one concern: survive what we encounter externally and survive what we carry internally. A person's ego develops from early childhood when they first start to realize their personhood (around seven months to a year old), and it continues to develop into the mid-20s. The ego helps reroute traffic, know when to run from danger, act in an emergency, and overall accomplish the necessary day-to-day tasks. The ego competes, worries, and suffers. The ego creates attachments to things like social media and video game narratives, especially the ones associated with power and affirmation, in order to co-opt these narratives to help people survive all that they carry inside: things like abandonment and unworthiness – common themes in the human experience - which come with their own narratives and belief systems. The ego also suppresses the painful experiences and emotions into the unconscious so that people do not have to continue feeling them. Our egos are meant to help us, but one of the primary tools of the ego is to suppress emotion, which can destroy our ability to experience true happiness and love for the sake of our survival. Why? As Brené Brown says, "You cannot selectively numb your emotions. When you numb the negative emotions, you also numb the beautiful ones."

Addiction:

Addiction has layers to it. And it functions very differently for kids than it does for adults. Let's define addiction as an unconscious attachment, created and protected by the ego, to an object, material/substance, experience, or narrative. Your child can't stop looking at Instagram (IG) not because of any particular conscious thought. The effect that IG has on your child registers on many levels of consciousness, but primarily on the level of the unconscious. And because it is in their unconscious, they inherently don't know it exists. Therefore, your kids don't believe or understand you when you tell them they are addicted to something. The ego blinds them to the attachments with believable narratives to justify/protect them from feeling the repressed pain and trauma that lies underneath all of it. This type of repressed (meaning "suppressed into the unconscious") emotional experience doesn't make your kids "not normal" in any way. It simply makes them human. So, in this guidebook, addiction refers to an unconscious attachment and helps us understand why all humans behave the way they do. Simply put, people have pain – even kids. Objects, materials/substances, experiences, and narratives become the medioation for that pain. Yes, you heard me correctly: Call of Duty can function as a drug, and a strong one at that.

Pain/The Human Condition:

A few things about being human are universal to all of us. In this quest to know how to help our kids navigate the ever-growing complexities of their world, we have to understand that they aren't any different than we are in this respect: they carry within their bodies a lifetime of stories and struggles to obtain the unconditional love that they need to thrive or even survive. And like us, they didn't have perfect parents that met every need they had. They experienced events that they didn't expect. They lost things. They got hurt. And as a result, they carry *pain* in their bodies. This is usually in the form of repressed emotional energy that gets stuck in the body instead of expressing itself and moving through and out of the body. So those knots that your child gets in his/her stomach? Those are old emotions – little sub-atomic particles packed into different spots in the body.

packed into different spots in the body. This ability to repress emotional pain within our bodies is the "human condition." We all learn how to do it in our childhood. Then we learn how to manage that pain with various forms of medication such as social media, gaming, substances, sex, work, and a myriad of other techniques the ego adopts for survival. But we all have pain. Our egos help us survive that pain. That survival instinct causes the most suffering in our lives.

Trigger:

So, if the human condition is the instinct to take all those negative emotions and stuff them down into the unconscious, what do we do when those emotions make a mess in our lives? Because they do. The unmet needs and anger and sadness that sits in our guts expresses itself from the unconscious. They put stress on relationships, demand medication, and cause all kinds of problems. The good news is that we can heal that pain by becoming aware of what hides deep down within us. Triggers bring awareness of repressed pain. You know someone is triggered when they have disproportionate emotional reactions to a situation. Think of panic attacks or simply consider this example:

> You tell your son that he can't play his video game until he cleans his room. He responds with anger as if you've tried to steal something from him. He attacks you with his words and snowballs into an emotional place that is hard to understand.

Or

> Your daughter has been on her phone for the last hour while you needed her help with something, and you find this anger rising inside of you that makes you want to get mean. You feel a tightness in your chest and try to not lash out.

Essentially, a *trigger* is when the repressed emotion a person has contained within them gets ignited. A trigger is a *gift* because it helps us locate and identify repressed emotional energy. We can know where it lives in the body, what it feels like, and even what it is really made of. A trigger provides a gateway to healing: that place where we can move the energy out of the body or transform it into something beautiful.

Awareness:

Typically, people use "awareness" to refer to that friend that has been in therapy for a while and has become very "self-aware," able to explain the source of their pain and probably give some good insight into your or your child's experience. They have a high level of self-awareness, which means they probably make decisions a little more consciously than some. Let's take awareness a step further. This guidebook fosters awareness of the things that trigger you in relationship to your kids and that awareness can guide you in how to connect to your kids in their experiences. And as that awareness rises, of course, then you can help nurture that same awareness in your kids as they invite you into that important and influential space we are desiring. Example:

> Your daughter posts a picture that's a little too grownup on her IG account, and you get annoyed. I mean, really annoyed. You stop and take a deep breath and discover a tight, achy knot in your chest. As you focus your attention on the knot, you start to recognize something deeper than just "annoyance." You might even recall some memories from your own childhood, including how you came to understand your own value. You suddenly realize that your daughter's action merely triggered some sort of old emotional energy, a wound of some sort, stuck in your chest.

As this type of awareness arises, we change. We can think and feel clearer because our unconscious baggage no longer grips us the same as it has. This gives us the ability to make decisions out of love and wisdom rather than fear and anxiety. And the truth is, far too many parents currently approach their kids' struggles by projecting their own deep fears and anxieties onto them.

This further propels them into an escapism that the world of technology happily facilitates. If our kids don't have to carry our baggage, they feel safer to come to us with their own.

With these definitions in mind, it's time to begin the process of raising awareness. Take some deep breaths and allow yourself to go slow and be present with each exercise. If you do, you will experience a shift that has the potential to change the life and direction of you and your kids.

How We Feel

" Feelings aroused by the touch of someone's hand, the sound of music, the smell of a flower, a beautiful sunset, a work of art, love, laughter, hope and faith - all work on both the unconscious and the conscious aspects of the self, and they have physiological consequences as well."

Bernie Siegel

" Feelings of worth can flourish only in an atmosphere where individual differences are appreciated, mistakes are tolerated, communication is open, and rules are flexible - the kind of atmosphere that is found in a nurturing family."

Virginia Satir

" I've learned that people will forget what you said, people will forget what you did, but people will never forget how you made them feel."

Maya Angelou

I have a friend who wrote a book about working with junior-high age kids, and when we talked about what motivates kids, she compared the way kids experience their world with crayons. She told me that before puberty, kids have that little 6 pack of simple emotions to color with, but when puberty hits, they suddenly have the 64 pack and the world gets brighter and more chaotic and harder to make sense of because they feel so much and have so little knowledge of what to do with all of it.

Some of those feelings they have are new, and some are old ones they have carried around with them for a long time. They are partly the little girl or boy you used to know, partly an emerging new creation, and partly some cybernetic being attached to a digital world that wants them to grow up even faster than they want to themselves...and far too fast in your view. Even the giving and receiving of love takes on a challenging complexity. But parents need to understand these complexities as an indication that kids feel *more* than they used to instead of *less*.

Feelings drive human beings. I may think that locking my car makes it safer, but really, it's the *feeling* of being safe that drives my actions. Even political and religious opinions reveal feelings regarding safety and value more so than thoughts or perceived intelligence. It often takes stillness and silence at a given moment to actually *feel those feelings*, and that lack of stillness in most of our lives is why we still perceive that we are driven by thoughts. We're moving too fast to feel. Though often labeled "sad" or "annoyed" or "angry," these feelings register mostly as physical sensations in the body because ultimately, feelings are energy — subatomic particles that carry a certain vibration and emotional signature.

Look at feeling "nervous". Perhaps your child has a performance of some sort. What do you feel before the event? You might say "I feel nervous." What does "nervous" feel like? You might say something like "I feel like rescuing my son/daughter from possible failure." This describes a thought, not a feeling. Again, what does wanting to rescue your child *feel* like? In your body, what do you actually feel? At this point, you might finally bring your attention to what's really going on below your neck. You may finally notice that the experience of "nervousness" is actually a response to a trigger. You feel knots in your stomach or a heaviness in your solar plexus. You feel energy uncomfortably stirring-up somewhere in your body. And now you can become aware of something that may have been with you for a long time. This trapped energy has long influenced you from its unconscious hiding place. In this way, the light of awareness can illuminate it, heal old hurts and bring growth. And when this awareness rises, we can see our kids with more love and less judgment. This then gives us a path forward to help our kids find similar awareness as they move into their adult years.

Some journaling exercises will help you explore these ideas. Taking your time and thoughtfully engaging with the exercises will give you a new level of awareness of how much feeling really goes on inside of you and your child. And this will give you a powerful new perspective regarding the actual role of social media and gaming in your child's world.

A Brief Note on Truth

Before digging into the experiential part of this book, let's compare knowing the facts and knowing the *truth*.

The wisest among us understand that understanding requires experience. No one knows this better than parents. All parents have had people without any children give them advice. Whether sound or not, receiving the advice is difficult because parenting is an *experience* as much, if not more, than it is a *skill*. For people who haven't felt their hearts beating outside of their body, like the Debra Ginsberg quote at the beginning of this book describes, how could they possibly know the truth of raising your child? They may know something that is *factually* accurate...but it lacks the truth spoken by someone who has experienced the trenches of diapers and sleep deprivation and strength of love beyond words.

The same actually goes for kids. Kids experience something adults don't understand fully, having *never* faced what they face. These exercises will intentionally and mindfully engage you in their daily experiences. Invest in the exercises and build a strong foundation to become a game-changing influence on your kids.

"Anything that's human is mention-able, and anything that is mention-able can be more manageable. When we can talk about our feelings, they become less overwhelming, less up-setting, and less scary. The people we trust with that important talk can help us know that we are not alone."

Fred Rogers

Exercise 1
Engage

The first thing is to engage with the activity that consumes your child. For social media, you might already be in that space. If your child has an IG account, then make sure you get one (or whatever platform that your child uses). Follow your child and follow several other accounts that interest you. Start making posts of your interests. The key is to engage with what interests you. When finished with this guidebook, feel free to delete it all if you wish.

If gaming is the issue, approach your child and ask them to teach you how to play the game. Spend enough time playing to really understand how the game is played. After engaging in these activities for a few hours, come back to the exercise and follow the instructions.

Don't begin to answer the following questions until you have a decent grasp on the specific medium that your kids are hooked into. Don't rush it – take time and seek to understand without judgement. If your answers run long, use the extra journaling space in the back of this book – just make note regarding what page you are continuing from and keep writing.

First, reflect on the narratives your child experiences. What stories do your kids hear about their identity, potential, and what makes them valuable and safe? Reflect deeply on the prominent narratives in your child's particular platform.

What do you experience in your body as you engage in the activity? Focus your attention on the feelings below your neck. Do you feel triggered? If so, where do you feel it? Describe your experience in detail. If you feel nothing, remember that the absence of feeling is a very distinct feeling. Make note of that without judgement.

Focusing on the concept of power, where does the narrative give power to your child? Contrast that to life experiences that may give your child a feeling, whether conscious or unconscious, of powerlessness. What type of balance does your child seek through these platforms?

Brainstorm: How might your child experience that same power/ powerlessness narrative balance without a digital platform? Think back to your childhood. What things made you feel empowered in your life? What people made you feel empowered and why?

Read back over what you just wrote. _If more thoughts come to mind,_
keep writing. Dive as deep as you can into these questions and reflec-
tions. These reflections on the stories our kids live and attempt to live will
provide you with insight and direction as you guide them towards a way of
living that has the power to transform them into the best version of them-
selves. With this perspective on what your child unconsciously feels and
receives from these platforms, you are ready to engage in deep, intentional,
and meaningful conversation with your child about their experience of their
world.

Exercise 2
Encounter

In this exercise, we're going to have an intentional conversation with your child. Clearly ask them for some time together and take them somewhere significant to them for a special meal or treat. A coffee shop could work great. Share honestly with your child that you want to ask them some serious questions and better understand their life experiences. Simply ask the questions, listen deeply, and write down their answers. During the conversation, breathe deeply and feel your body's reactions to their answers.

Ask any clarifying or follow-up questions with true curiosity and without judgement. Attaching judgement, defensiveness, or the need to instruct to the questions will disrupt the goal of the exercise. This is about building trust and understanding with the ultimate goal of being invited into a deeply sacred and influential space in your child's life. Just staying as present as possible and not going to war with their obsessions will create a productive time together. Establish that right from the beginning, ask them the questions, write/reflect. Make it feel like an interview, as if you're writing a newspaper story about them. Remember – breathe deeply and observe your body's experiences while they answer.

What do you love the most about (insert social media platform or video game[s])? Why this particular (insert social media platform or video game[s])? (If the answer is "I don't know," just be present (calm, curious, and open) and ask them to really think about it, giving them space in which to do so. Your curiosity can spark their curiosity. Ask any follow-up questions you need to in order to understand them.)

How do you feel when you play/surf/post (insert social media platform or video game[s])? (Things like "I feel powerful" or "I like it" are thoughts rather than feelings. They have likely never thought about their feelings much. Ask them to reflect if they don't know. Don't push them anywhere. Maybe talk about what you experience in your body while you engage in it to help them understand. Ex: "I feel intense energy, like excitement, in my chest.")

I want to understand better what you experience in your life. How do you think I misunderstand your experiences of things like (insert social media platform or video game[s])? (Remember to breathe deeply and remain curious. Receive their experience and validate it.)

If you were in my shoes, what would you do to help your child/ teenager live a balanced and healthy life in regard to digital media? Give me at least three things. (Remember this is about understanding – so breathe deeply.)

Let these questions fuel your conversation but remember that if you feel some need in your body to interject your agenda or defend yourself, take a deep breath and pull it back. Allow them to not understand what you want them to understand, for now. This chapter of your relationship is about building trust and a loving connection.

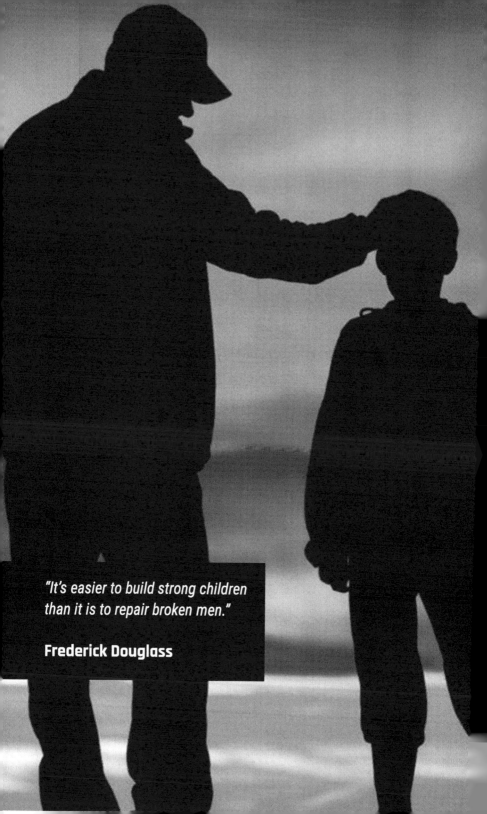

"It's easier to build strong children than it is to repair broken men."

Frederick Douglass

The Courage to Trust

It takes a lot of courage to trust that our kids have the capacity to find their way through the fog of adolescence. Sometimes parents struggle to trust that they have adequately prepared their children. And sometimes parents just get sucked into the dominant group-think that the negative influences in the world are just too strong.

But what if the nature of transformation reveals the deepest and truest parts of people through struggle? If so, your child's unique journey requires guidance as opposed to opposition. And their desire for this thing they obsess over pales in comparison to the love and affirmation they desire from you. Their need and desire for your love might live at a mostly unconscious level at this period and kids lack the adult capacity for self-awareness, so you might not always experience their desire for your love. But if you value their love nonetheless and treat them with deep respect, you will experience less fear of their experience or addiction. Essentially, your child has time to find balance, and their journey is important. Don't go to war with it – engage with them intentionally. Shallow things like games and social media don't cause the real damage to kids; distance and denial from their source of love, however, do.

Exercise 3
Experience

You might have noticed by now that these exercises start to repro-
gram you (followed by your child) to *feel* rather than merely think.
People are feeling creatures. People process the world through
feeling every second of every day, even while sleeping. But the ego,
in charge of your survival, works constantly to manage every challenge you face, especially that which lives repressed in your unconscious. The ego's main tool is the brain – the thinking mind. Most
people think too much. Raising awareness begins with an intentional
practice of feeling. It's a tricky thing to learn how to do. Some people
find that running or going to the gym connects them to their body
and feeling, but the ego often co-opts activities like that to control
emotion further.

Many spiritual traditions teach meditation, stillness, contemplation,
or time in nature as the way to feeling. Modern psychology also af-
firms that silence and stillness has the capacity to transform our experience everyday into a healthier way of being. In the next exercise,
you're going to practice feeling the contrast between the disconnec-
tion of the ego and the deep connection of your true-self: the part of
you that lives in the moment and feels empowered because it knows
that everything is ok. You simply need weather-appropriate clothing,
about an hour of free time, and a cell phone. Leave this book behind,
but make sure you understand the directions completely before you
go.

For this exercise, go into nature. Anything wild will do: go on a hike,
get on a beach or some water. The quieter, the better. Invite your
child to go with you, and if they accept, explain the exercise. If they
refuse, just know you're meant to do this alone. Begin the experience, whether walking, rowing, sitting, etc. with feeling your body's
sensations as much as you can. Feel your environment. Feel the air
around you. Breathe deeply. Observe the trees or water or mountains
or garden. Observe your body's reaction to these things. If thoughts
interrupt, observe these also. Do this for at least 15-20 minutes.

Next, pull out your cell phone and engage with social media or play a game for five minutes. Observe yourself. Feel your body's reaction to the digital experience. Do you feel more connected to your environment and body or less? Describe it to yourself. Now put the phone down and return your attention to nature for 15 minutes. Observe the connection to your environment and body that you felt before; is it still present, unchanged, or different? Do you *think* or do you *feel* "in your body." Return to your phone again. Feel the contrasting experience. After five more minutes, return your attention to nature again and observe how the time on your phone affects you and your relationship and connection to your environment.

When you return to this book, write your observations of the experience. Reflect on what just happened and what your child needs to experience in light of this. Through feeling, your kids will truly experience their world. How can we as parents help them feel, ground, and balance in a world that increasingly teaches them how to live inside of artificial constructs managed by the thinking mind?

Observations

The next exercises may not be as emotional but are just as important in understanding so many of the factors that shape your kids' world every day.

"The best and most beautiful
things in the world cannot be seen
or even touched. They must be
felt with the heart."

Helen Keller

How We Think

"As a single footstep will not make a path on the earth, so a single thought will not make a pathway in the mind. To make a deep physical path, we walk again and again. To make a deep mental path, we must think over and over the kind of thoughts we wish to dominate our lives."

Wilfred Arlan Peterson

"The closer you come to knowing that you alone create the world of your experience, the more vital it becomes for you to discover just who is doing the creating."

Eric Micha'el Leventhal

"Each of us has more intelligence than we are trained to use and the part that we get graded on in school doesn't amount to much."

Laurie Nadel

When I was a child, you could bet that, at any given moment, very smart people were hard at work to figure out how to get my little brain to want what they had to sell. Saturday morning for my siblings and me was all about watching cartoons on our tiny television, and we loved the commercials as much as the cartoons themselves. We loved watching the ultimate, adrenaline-filled adventure of the kids playing with the Transformers or GI Joes in the commercial. And every commercial ended with a statement like, "I want that!"

When I take my kids to any store, everything they see prompts them to ask me for things at a rate of nearly one request every five seconds. "I want that!" they exclaim with a passion that only a child can bring.

When my wife and I go to the movies, I love to watch the trailers for the upcoming films. After each one, we look at each other with either a look of disinterest or an enthusiastic, "I want to see that!"

The human race has an awe-inspiring appetite for consumption. Understanding how and why kids consume what they consume is essential to becoming a creative and intentional parent capable of providing balance.

The commercial realm constantly puts out a huge volume of messages. In this section, we are going to attempt to become *fully* aware of all the stuff that slips past your adult consciousness. And we're going to become curious about how much more of these things our kids soak in from minute to minute – all of it brought to them brilliantly and at hyper speed? As our awareness of this subconscious blitzkrieg grows and our understanding of how it impacts us expands, we will be more empowered by the minute to bring balance to the lives of our kids and ourselves.

"The essential question we must constantly ask ourselves in the quickly evolving age of digital technology is not what can I do with my phone, but what should I do with it? That answer...can be resolved only by understanding why we exist in the first place."

Tony Reinke, author of 12 Ways Your Phone is Changing You

Exercise 1
Remember When

This exercise may feel like a classic top-3 list. Think for a bit about your top-3 favorite commercials from your life. Let your mind drift back to memories from your childhood. Describe the product and the presentation. Write as much as you can regarding *why* you loved it. ***Did the commercial work?*** The answer to that question could be complex. Maybe you simply bought the product. But maybe it sank deeper. Perhaps you hatched a lifelong fantasy, either conscious, unconscious, or both, about a certain dream car. (Certain truck commercials from my childhood later led to me buying a hard-core, off-road truck.) Maybe you became a "Nike person" or something like that. Trace the path that these messages travelled through your consciousness. This could be both fun and illuminating as to how marketing messages have affected you.

Commercial Title:

Ranking

Enter number from 3 to 1

Commercial Description:

Why do you love it?

Did it work?

Commercial Title:

Ranking

Enter number from 3 to 1

Commercial Description:

Why do you love it?

Did it work?

Commercial Title:

Ranking

Enter number from 3 to 1

Commercial Description:

Why do you love it?

Did it work?

Exercise 2
Interview Part Deux

Return to the special coffee shop or whatever is your kid's designated special spot. Ask your child to join you again for a discussion. Put on your best TV show host hat and ask the same questions from the last exercise. What is their top-5 commercials? Share with them your top 3. Share why you loved them and ask your child about why they love the ones they love. If you get a short answer, dig deeper like a good interviewer. Ask them to think more about it. Then ask them if the commercials "worked" on them. Talk about your experience with that question. No need to write down all of the information that they give you but write down their answer regarding *who they are and how they view the world*. Simply have a great conversation with your kid about the everyday deluge of messaging. Get a deeper understanding of your child's identity and thought process.

Observations

Observations

War Creates War

It's important that we resist going to war with the technological juggernaut that shapes the universe. Your power exists in accepting the world as it is. Fighting the current of the multi-billion-dollar river through judgement and constant wrestling creates kids that learn to repress their desires and label them as evil, and they don't grow. Or it creates kids that simply rebel against their parents' love and authority and learn lessons in an unnecessarily hard way.

Instead, if you can put some faith in the power of love and understanding, you help create kids that can take some risks, see themselves more clearly, learn from mistakes, and most importantly, aren't afraid to talk to you about what matters to them. As they move into adulthood, that trust becomes priceless.

Exercise 3
The Balance in the Force

Section 1 of this guidebook discussed the effect that social media and gaming narratives have on kids. Beauty, value, and power (which equals love) overwhelmingly color the experience that kids have in artificial experience platforms. The companies that sell this stuff recognize that getting kids hooked simply requires providing them with small doses of balance in how they feel about themselves – doses that fade quickly so as to keep them coming back. Companies recognize that most kids, at least at subtle unconscious levels, feel ugly, undervalued, and powerless (which equals unloved). Most human beings, regardless of age, feel this way. No matter how good the parents or life, people still have a hole in them somewhere: often referred to as "The Human Condition." Some people experience it in much harsher ways than others. Growth requires accepting the human experience. In the final exercise of Section 2 - How We Think, we will engage in learning to step in and provide balance for your kids in ways that the tech-exec-blob can't.

In this exercise, we are going to simply start creatively sending messages of love, beauty power, and acceptance to your child. Messages like this must always be backed with actions, in the same way that platforms like Instagram do. Instagram defines beauty and delivers filters and selfie sticks and photo editing for people to use to fit into that definition. These actions anchor the message into your child's consciousness. Kids can cry from heartbreak one second and showcase their happiness in a perfectly crafted photo the next. And of course, their "friends" can immediately send them digital approval: likes, hearts, sad-face emojis, etc. These small doses of love get packaged and delivered at the drop of a hat. So, in order for the next exercise to work, action must anchor the message, not just words.

My friend Emily still talks about when she was a girl, all the way up through high school, her Dad occasionally hid little green army men in her lunches, backpacks, and school supplies. Not because he was a soldier or because Emily particularly liked playing with army figures. But her Dad understood that it would stand out. It sent a message on a brilliant level; whenever she found a figurine, she received a very powerful message of love and affection, no matter what else happened. She knew her dad was thinking about her that day. And he backed up those messages by spending time with her on weekends, talking without judging her adolescent problems as trivial, and instead compassionately accepting and validating her experience.

My wife often puts a handwritten message of love in my daughter's lunch, always referring to her as "Mom's wildflower." She takes her into the woods at least once a week and grounds her in the love of the forest by putting the phone away and being present, even if they only have 30 minutes.

My brother and I obsessed over baseball cards when we were young, so my dad started collecting them. He came to the shop with us and taught us about value and money through baseball cards. And we started to go to more games together, too. He joined us in our passion and in that, provided something much more powerful than any corporate message could.

Put your creative hat on. Outline three creative ideas to introduce your love as the balancing force in your child's obsessions. At the top of the page, write a title for the idea (i.e. "Hidden Army Men Love Takeover" or "The Hour of Adventure"). Then write down the concept. Finally, write down an act of love that you can perform consistently to anchor those messages into your child's consciousness.

Idea:

Details of Idea:

_____

_____

_____

_____

_____

_____

_____

_____

_____

Anchoring Action Step:

_____

_____

_____

_____

_____

_____

_____

_____

_____

_____

_____

Idea:

Details of Idea:

_____

_____

_____

_____

_____

_____

_____

_____

Anchoring Action Step:

_____

_____

_____

_____

_____

_____

_____

_____

_____

_____

_____

Idea:

Details of Idea:

Anchoring Action Step:

"Never underestimate the infinite love within you. It has the power to transform lives."

Mimi Novic , The Silence Between the Sighs

Section 3

How We Act

"Success is not final, failure is not fatal: it is the courage to continue that counts."
Winston S. Churchill

"I wanted you to see what real courage is, instead of getting the idea that courage is a man with a gun in his hand. It's when you know you're licked before you begin, but you begin anyway and see it through no matter what.
- Atticus Finch."
Harper Lee, To Kill a Mockingbird

"Confront the dark parts of yourself, and work to banish them with illumination and forgiveness. Your willingness to wrestle with your demons will cause your angels to sing."
August Wilson

I've been coaching soccer for many years and recently, I went to a soccer practice of a friend of mine who plays professionally to observe his play and help him with some of his internal experience. I noticed certain interesting patterns of how he moved around the field during the game, and I decided to ask him about it afterwards. I showed him on a sketchpad the types of runs/movements he kept making.

"Here's what you should have done. Here's what you did...here's what you should have done, here's what you did," I said several times as I drew on the sketchpad. The pattern became obvious to him as I spoke.

"What does that look like to you?" I asked.

"I'm hiding," he replied. His movements were all to the safer areas on the field, away from the action.

"Yes," I said with a smile. "Let me ask you something about your experience out there. Are you *doing* anything to this game or is the game just happening to you?"

"It's just happening to me," he replied after some thought. "Everything is a reaction...nothing is intentional."

"Yes," I nodded in agreement. In that moment, he had a revelation about the level of **consciousness** that dictated his life, not just his game. He played soccer asleep. But why? Why did he seem to be run by an unconscious drive towards safety rather than a bold willingness to take risk and push forward, which was clearly the more productive action for his soccer career?

With this revelation, he went back in the game with the intention of *doing something to the game*. And he did. He put himself in dangerous positions and started to bang around in the center of the action. When he came out next, he clutched his chest and breathed hard. He hadn't run that hard, but he was struggling to breathe. His risk-taking had triggered some form of repressed

64

emotional energy in his chest. Playing in the center of the action, he risked struggle and failure. And this courageous action raised some part of his deep unconscious to the surface. And now the opportunity to move towards healing presented itself. So, he took it and started doing important therapeutic work on a weekly basis. To this day, he's playing better than ever before and enjoying himself more.

Intentional living breeds transformation.

Intentional parenting gets tougher as kids get older, because they seem increasingly able to take care of themselves. The complexity of their internal lives grows, and they hide more and more of their thoughts and feelings inside of themselves. Addictive media platforms facilitate that shadow element very effectively. It is a parents' job to facilitate an experience for their kids that allows the light to shine in as much as possible.

Curiosity and courage become the two most important elements to possess in this adventure. Curiosity overcomes judgement, courage overcomes apathy and fear. With these two characteristics as a way of life, parents can risk intentional and creative action in their kids' lives. And that can help balance their kids' lives as they learn how to grab the steering wheel of life and head out onto the highway.

In the final section of the guidebook, let your curiosity and courage manifest creativity, and see what kind of new paths you can create for the life of your family.

"Have enough courage to trust love one more time and always one more time."
Maya Angelou

Exercise 1
Learning from the Past

You were a kid once. You went through the same things your child goes through, only with a different environment and cultural climate around you. You also probably have moments where you find yourself repeating to your child what your parents said to you. By now, you probably have made some of the same mistakes that they made with you. And you might have improved on some of what your parents did. This exercise is about identifying some of your remaining programming and examining the elements of it that help and the ones that hinder.

In this exercise, you're going to identify three things your parents did in dealing with your emerging identity, independence, and mistakes/problems/struggles. The ones that stick out in your memory most likely hurt the most, but perhaps some created more space, trust, and beauty in your relationship. Don't rush. Let the memories surface and honor the pain or pleasure that comes with them. Write down your struggles, your parent's reactions, and what you wish they had done. After completing this activity five separate times, reflect on the parallels between what your parents did and what you do. Where do you see similar fears or anxieties? Where do you see similar successes? How does your child's connection to Social Media or gaming parallel some of your childhood obsessions?

Memory 1

What my parents did:

Memory 1

What I wish they had done:

Memory 2

What my parents did:

Memory 2

What I wish they had done:

Memory 3

What my parents did:

What I wish they had done:

What parallels do you see in your experience with your child? Where do you find yourself echoing your parents? How is that hurting? How is that helping?"

Exercise 2
Do Be Do Be Do...

Deepak Chopra describes the key to life as the dance between Doing and Being. The mind drives the *doing* of life. We do so much processing in the brain and some of it is necessary. You use the brain, the thinking mind, to go to work, pay bills, drive a car and survive each day. But the good stuff, the *being*, experienced as joy and happiness and connection, happens in the body and comes from the soul. In the best moments of your life, the excitement and the pleasure, time seems to stand still, and we feel it all in the deepest parts of ourselves. And because those moments make life worth living, we end up in the *doing*, so we can just spend more time in the *being*.

Children spend a lot of time *doing,* but not much time *being*. One critical role parents can play in a child's life is to bring balance to the *doing* and *being*. In this exercise, think of some creative things to *do*, and consider how those actions can help you and your child just be. This can teach us what it means to live a life of balance. You don't need to take gaming and social media away from your child; instead, you can play a part in waking up the part of them that desires a healthy balance in their life. Because at some deep and possibly hidden level inside of them, they crave balance and love and health, just like everyone else.

When my wife writes a hand-written note of love for my daughter each day, she's in the doing part of herself. This *doing* facilitates an experience of *being* with my daughter that reinforces those messages. When my daughter blows her top over something and my wife patiently allows the tantrum to move through her, sitting with her intense emotions without having to *fix* anything, my daughter feels the truth of the messages. In those moments, my wife and my daughter just *be*. I, on the other hand, have a difficult time *being* with my daughter. I'm good at the *doing* – I give her messages of love all day long – but I struggle with her expression of more negative emotions. As I have identified my struggle to *be* with my daughter's emotions, I have learned a great deal about myself. I've found pain from my own childhood and my parents' struggles in *being* with my negative emotions. I've grown in my ability to be with my own negative emotions in a loving way. And out of that growth, my daughter then experiences more of my presence and less of my judgment.

In this exercise, you're going to write down three creative ideas that you can do to deliver messages and experiences of love and balance to your child. For each act of *doing*, write an experience where you might exercise *being*.

> **Example: At least once a week, I play my son's video game with him. As I learn to be with him without judgement, he trusts me more and reacts well when I ask him to come hike with me at least once a week. When we hike, we talk about being, and I intentionally allow space for the questions coming up for him, and try to move the conversation away from the performance-oriented parts of his life. This creates a ritual of balance and depth in our relationship.**

Remember as you do this, non-judgement is the most important part of *being*. Holding to an agenda will break trust instead of building it, because children will sniff it out in a heartbeat.

Idea #1

Doing:

Idea #1

How can I be with my child as a result of this doing?

Idea #2

Doing:

How can I be with my child as a result of this doing? ....

Idea #3

Doing:

How can I **be** with my child as a result of this **doing?**

Reflecting on personal childhood experiences and interacting with your child in light of these reflections, two major themes tend to emerge for most parents despite how old they might be: pain and programming. Both your pain and your programming dictate a great deal of your parenting. Both can make it difficult to truly be present with your kids. But as you gain awareness, you will be empowered to turn some serious attention to the healing of your pain and a deeper examination of your programming. That healing and examination increases your preparedness to launch your kids into a deeply complex adult world, and also joyfully enter the next chapter in your own life as you reorient yourself to your own desires and goals.

Starting with any type of therapy can hugely impact your relationship with your child as you move towards mental, emotional, and spiritual health in your own life. Other methods for healing include building daily practices like meditation, spending time in nature, and getting better sleep. Each person has a unique path, but the journey begins with a step.

"...People are rivers, always ready to move from one state of being into another. It is not fair, to treat people as if they are finished beings. Everyone is always becoming and unbecoming."
Kathleen Winter, Annabel

Exercise 3
Setting Your Intention

In this exercise, you are going to practice setting intentions. Intentions are not promises you make to yourself – promises break easily. Intentions are desires you have that you decide are going to be fulfilled. You may not know how, but you decide that you are wide open to these desires becoming a reality in your life by any means necessary. Intentions are directed outward into the Universe with hope. And intentions are not something we grip tightly or try to control. We simply set them and then watch for opportunities to take small steps towards their outcome.

Go ahead and write for a while about changes you want in your life and the life of your family. The fact that you picked up this book shows that you want change in your life. Even though you may have started out to change your child, perhaps you now realize that helping other people change requires showing them the way. What do you want to be? And how will it affect the life of your child?

Write answers to each of the following questions. Think back to the lessons so far. Think about the road ahead as a parent, and imagine what it could look like. Breathe deeply and be present as you write. Do not rush.

What is your intention for your child's experience of your relationship? What do you want it to look like? What do you want it to feel like? What are you prepared to do to bring this about?

Think ahead 5 years. What is your intention for your child's experience of your relationship 5 years from now. What do you want them to carry from day to day because of their experience of being raised by you?

What is your intention for your internal life from day to day? What do you want to experience in your body? Your mind? Your emotions? What are one or two steps you can take immediately to move towards making this the reality? (ex: start a meditation practice – engage a therapist)

What is your intention for your experience of your child's passions, interests, and even obsessions? Do you intend to fight a war with them or begin to creatively engage with them? How do you want your child to remember this time of their lives in regard to how you engaged their desires?

"Intention is one of the most powerful forces there is. What you mean when you do a thing will always determine the outcome. The law creates the world."

Brenna Yovanoff, The Re-placement

Conclusion

A Bold New World

"Life can only be understood backwards; but it must be lived forwards."
Søren Kierkegaard

"Do not let the memories of your past limit the potential of your future. There are no limits to what you can achieve on your journey through life, except in your mind."
Roy T. Bennett, The Light in the Heart

"I'm choosing happiness over suffering, I know I am. I'm making space for the unknown future to fill up my life with yet-to-come surprises."
Elizabeth Gilbert, Eat, Pray, Love

You probably remember well the days when your kids wanted to cuddle in the morning and loved being held in your arms. But just because children grow and don't want to cuddle anymore, and the world seems to steal them away a little more each day, doesn't diminish the magic of watching them grow and live. You simply may have to just look harder for it. It may require more of your focus to see it. The nature of a child's growth has a role in maturing parents in the process. The growth requires intentional, courageous, honest, humble, and strong parents. And that is difficult. Parents often yearn for the days when caring for their children simply meant changing a diaper or helping them brush their teeth. Adolescents don't need parents for any of that. But do they need parents still?

Yes, of course they do. They need their parents even more.

The challenges kids face, and the gap that platforms like gaming and social media fill to "help" them can feel overwhelmingly beyond the comfort zones of most parents. But again, nothing in this world holds a candle to your love for your child. Your love has the power to hold your child together as they prepare to face the storms of life. They will return to your love repeatedly throughout life, facing challenge after challenge long after obsessions with social media and gaming have faded into oblivion.

Children need Sages, not Saints. They need mentors, not just parents. They need you to allow yourself to be more and more *human*. Hopefully this experience helped you find a little more of your humanity and perhaps even a little more of the Superhuman within you. On behalf of the world in which you live and the children which you must love and raise, thank you for engaging in this process.

A friend of mine named Mike Schatz came to me one day and said, "Hey, you know those guidebooks you make? I think parents could really use some help with what to do about their kids hooked into digital media. It's a nightmare." And thus, this project was born. Mike's idea, Mike's funding, Mike's desire to help parents like himself who's kids are being blitzed every day at a rate that is mind-blowing. Most of the credit goes to him.

Thanks to Josiah Hampton for some great editing and writing help and to the wonderful Nataly Efremowa for her killer design chops. Thanks also to my brother David who, as always, is there with his wisdom and vast experience in writing and design to open my eyes and mind.

We all hope that this guidebook adds some beauty and life to this world we love.

Seth

"We shall not cease from exploration
And the end of all our exploring
Will be to arrive where we started
And know the place for the first time."

**T.S. Eliot,
Four Quartets**

Notes

Notes

Notes

Notes

Notes

Notes

Notes

Made in the USA
Lexington, KY
09 January 2019